Hurricane!

By MARY MĀDEN

#6 In A Series

PUBLISHED IN THE U.S.A. by DOG AND PONY ENTERPRISES
P.O. Box 3540, Kill Devil Hills, NC 27948
Library of Congress Catalog Card Number: 97-66747 ISBN: 1-890479-51-9

It was a hot summer day. Petey and Tazz were spending the whole day at the beach. They were having a wonderful time.

"Wow! This sure is fun," said Petey, paddling around in the water. "I love the ocean!"

"For sure," agreed Tazz, relaxing on a float.

Tazz's float bobbed lazily on top of the waves like a cork.

"Let's bodysurf," suggested Petey.

"Later . . ." said Tazz, still relaxing.

Just then, Petey spotted a group of dolphins swimming by.

"Hey, Dolly!" called Petey to a dolphin in the group. The little dolphin swam over.

"Hi, Petey! Hi, Tazz!" greeted Dolly Dolphin.

"Come join us," invited Petey. "We're having a great time!"

"I'd like to," said Dolly, "but I can't right now. Auntie said I must stay close by. There may be a hurricane coming!"

"Dolly! Come along!" scolded Auntie Dolphin. "We must be on our way."

"Yes, Auntie!" called Dolly. "Sorry, guys. I have to go. See you later!"

Dolly headed back to Auntie and the other dolphins.

"Keep a watch out for hurricanes!" warned Dolly as she swam away.

"Wow! A hurricane may be coming," Petey looked puzzled, then asked, "what is a hurricane?"
"Well, Petey My Boy," replied Tazz, "you know . . . we have them sometimes. A hurricane is a . . . er, that is . . . well, it's a . . . ."
". . . terrible, churning, spinning, swirling mass of destruction!" shouted a deep voice.
Tazz was so startled, he flipped right off his float!
"Gustav Horatio P. Pelican here," announced the voice. "But you may call me Old Gus!"
Petey and Tazz looked up and saw a great brown pelican.

Old Gus settled himself on a piling. "You're in luck!" he said. "I am **the** expert on the subject of tropical cyclones also known by the names hurricane, cyclone, typhoon — or as they are called in Australia — willy-willies."

Petey and Tazz came over to listen, eager to hear more.

"Now, we call a tropical cyclone a **hurricane** in these parts. But whatever you choose to call them — they are awesome storms!" said Old Gus.

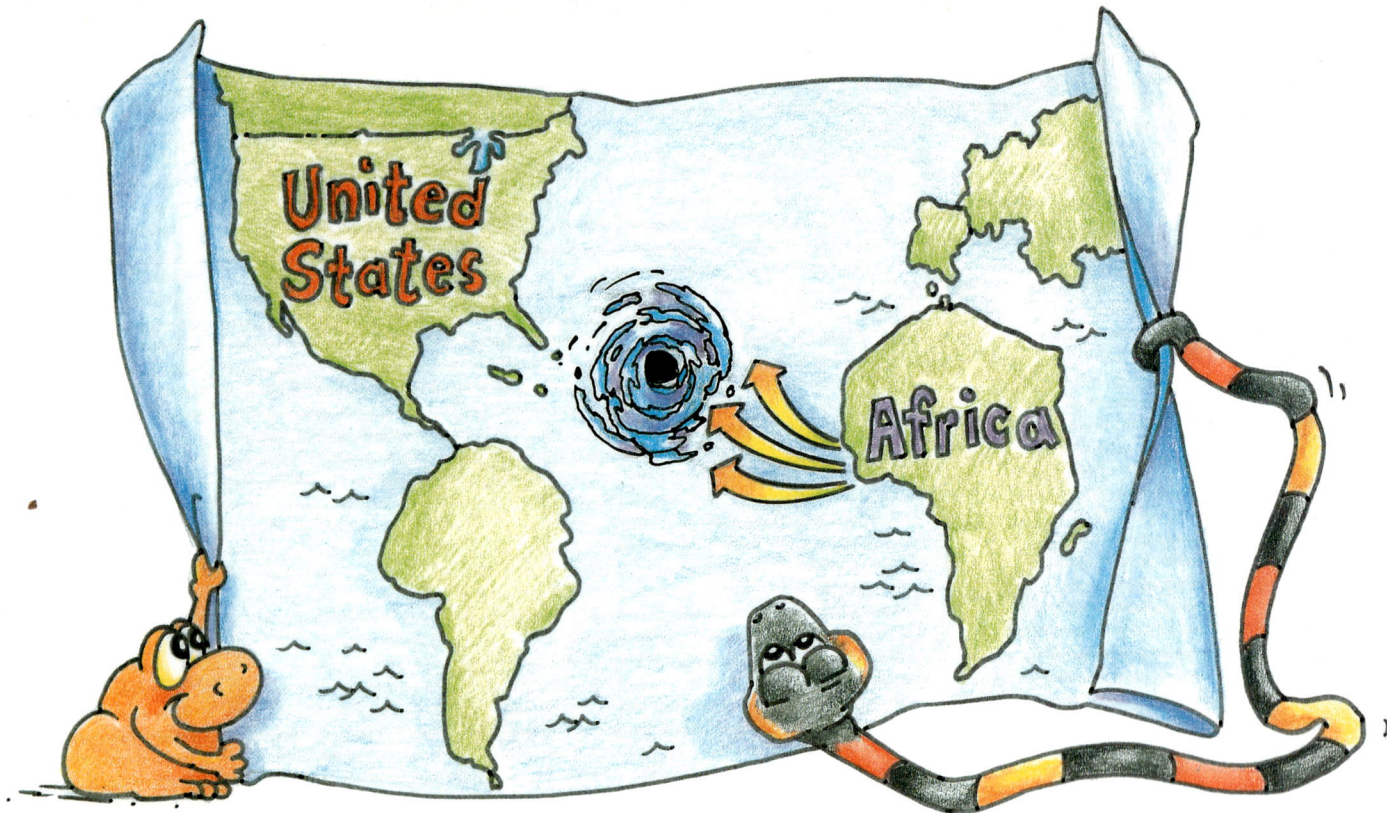

"Tell us some more about hurricanes!" begged Petey and Tazz.

"Well, let's see now . . . a hurricane is a funny kind of storm," Old Gus began.

"A hurricane spins in a circle and moves forward — all at the same time!"

Old Gus continued, "Hurricanes are huge, too — hundreds of miles wide. These monster storms form over warm tropical waters near the equator. Hurricanes can move hundreds of miles in a single day."

"Do hurricanes move in a straight line?" asked Petey.

"No. They wobble," answered Old Gus. "They usually move slowly at first, only 10-20 miles an hour. But they can speed up quickly and move as fast as 70 miles an hour! One thing is for sure — the movement of a hurricane is hard to predict!"

"You said that hurricanes spin in a circle . . ." Petey reminded Old Gus.

"They sure do," said Old Gus. "Hurricanes have very strong winds that move in a spiral counterclockwise around the eye."

"Hurricanes don't have eyes!" snorted Tazz in disbelief.

"The center of the hurricane is called the eye," explained Old Gus.

"The eye of a hurricane is a strange, eerie thing," continued Old Gus. "When it passes over, everything gets real quiet and calm. The wind dies down. You can see the blue sky. Why, the sun even shines!"

"When the eye passes across, is the hurricane over?" asked Petey.

"No! That's a dangerous thing to think," warned Old Gus. "After the eye passes, the winds change direction and pick back up again."

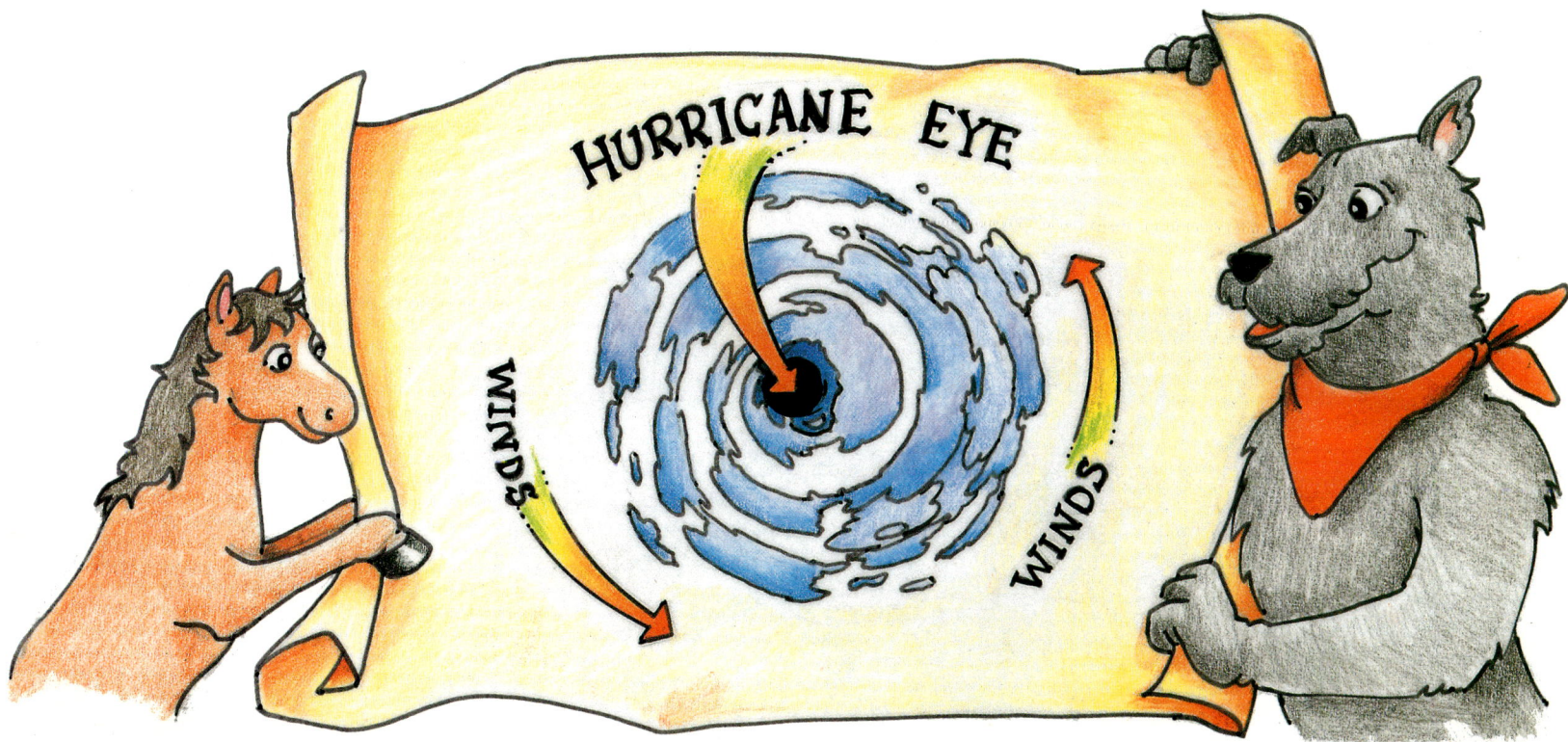

"Is the wind the worst part of the hurricane?" asked Petey.

"The winds are dangerous, sure enough," answered Old Gus, "but the storm surge and high tides can be even worse."

"Yep," said Tazz, "a big, giant tidal wave comes in and . . . ."

"It's not like that," corrected Old Gus. "When a hurricane hits the coast, the water level rises higher than normal. A large dome of water called the storm surge comes ashore. High waves sweep the shore over a period of time — not in one giant wave! People have been known to find fish in their furniture and crabs in their beds after storm tides have washed through their homes!"

"I'll tell you a little known fact," confided Old Gus. "I know when a hurricane's coming."
"Wow!" said Petey, impressed. "How do you know that?"
"Well, I don't need any new-fangled equipment like those Weather Service boys," bragged Old Gus. "They use all kinds of fancy doo-dads — computers, radar, satellites, airplanes, and such." Old Gus chuckled and shook his head. "Why, they even fly those airplanes straight into hurricanes! You won't catch me flying into a hurricane — at least not on purpose. I do recall a time, though, when my cousin Henry got caught in the eye of a hurricane . . . ."
"You were going to tell us how you know when a hurricane's coming," interrupted Tazz.
"I was gettin' to that," continued Old Gus. "When a hurricane's coming, I get the feeling."
"What's that?" asked Petey.
"I don't rightly know," answered Old Gus. "The feeling just kinda comes over me. The closer the hurricane gets — the stronger the feeling gets!"

"I even have my own system of rating hurricanes," said Old Gus. "I call it the Suffering Hurricane Scale."

"How does it work?" asked Petey.

"Well, you see, I can tell how strong a hurricane is by how much my bones ache," Old Gus explained. "When a hurricane is coming, my rheumatism acts up something fierce. The worse I hurt — the worse the hurricane is."

Suffering Scale

Category 1:
Sustained Winds
74-95 m.p.h.
Not much damage

Category 2:
Sustained Winds
96-110 m.p.h.
Pretty much damage

Category 3:
Sustained Winds
111-130 m.p.h.
Lots of damage

Category 4:
Sustained Winds
131-155 m.p.h.
Terrible damage

Category 5:
Sustained Winds
+156 m.p.h.
Awesome damage

"Tell us about the scale," said Petey and Tazz.

"First on the scale is a Category 1 hurricane," began Old Gus. "My little toe aches when a Category 1 is coming. Hurricane Charley was a Category 1. He hit the Outer Banks of North Carolina in 1988. Next is a Category 2. My big toe hurts something terrible when there's a Category 2 hurricane. Hurricane Bob in 1991 was a Category 2."

"Are Category 1's and 2's dangerous?" asked Petey.

"Any hurricane can be dangerous," explained Old Gus. "Agnes was only a Category 1 hurricane, but caused terrible flooding and destruction back in 1972."

"There's a Category 1 and a Category 2 . . ." mumbled Tazz, "so next is a . . . er . . . ."

"A Category 3!" shouted Petey.

"I knew that," mumbled Tazz, counting on his fingers.

"Right! A Category 3 is a major hurricane," explained Old Gus. "My whole foot hurts when a Category 3 is on its way. Hurricane Emily was a Category 3. She hit Hatteras, North Carolina, pretty hard back in 1993."

"Did Emily do a lot of damage?" questioned Petey.

"A fair amount," answered Old Gus. "Emily's fierce winds ripped off the tops of houses and snapped big pine trees in two. The flooding was bad. Four feet of water filled the local school. Emily left behind a real, big mess to clean up!"

"What's next on the scale?" asked Petey.

"A Category 4," answered Old Gus. "A Category 4 is one mean hurricane! All my toes and both my feet hurt when a Category 4 is brewing."

"Is a Category 4 hurricane dangerous?" whispered Tazz.

"A Category 4 is a very serious storm," answered Old Gus. "Why, just the mention of some Category 4's like Hazel, Hugo, and Andrew give me the willies!"

"Do you remember those hurricanes?" asked Petey.

"I'll never forget them! I was just a young pelican when Hazel tore through, but I remember it like it was yesterday . . ." began Old Gus.

"It was in the morning, on October 15, 1954, when Hazel struck the coast," remembered Old Gus. "She came inland near the North Carolina-South Carolina border — and she didn't stop until she reached the Arctic Circle!"

"Wow!" gasped Petey and Tazz, eyes wide in amazement.

"Hurricanes usually weaken when they move over land," said Old Gus, "but not Hazel! She smashed into the helpless coast washing away trees, houses, cars — even a drawbridge. And she kept going. Hazel blew north all the way into Canada! The whole way the vicious hurricane blew down trees, power lines, and ripped the roofs off houses. Heavy rains caused dangerous floods. Hurricane Hazel left a path of death and destruction 2,000 miles long!"

"Do hurricanes like Hazel happen a lot?" asked Petey, worried.

"Not too often," assured Old Gus. "But Category 4 hurricanes do strike. Hurricanes like Hugo in 1989 and Andrew in 1992!"

"What were they like?" questioned Petey and Tazz.

"They were some bad boys!" answered Old Gus. "Hugo devastated the Charleston, South Carolina, area. He came screaming in around midnight with 130 mile an hour winds and huge tides. One story goes that a fisherman rode out the storm in his boat. He said he floated right over the tops of houses!"

THE ERIC

Old Gus shook his head sadly and continued, "Hugo did a lot of damage, but Andrew did even more. Andrew caused 25 billion dollars worth of damage!"

"Wow! I can't even count that high!" exclaimed Petey.

"Hurricane Andrew struck Florida near Homestead Air Force Base. Andrew was even felt at the National Hurricane Center! Andrew's winds gusted near 175 miles an hour. Bad boy Andrew wiped out whole neighborhoods. It was awful! Finally, he headed back to sea."

"Boy, I bet everyone was glad Andrew went away!" said Petey.

"But," continued Old Gus, leaning close, "he came back! Andrew regained his strength. He headed back inland toward Louisiana and did damage there before he was through."

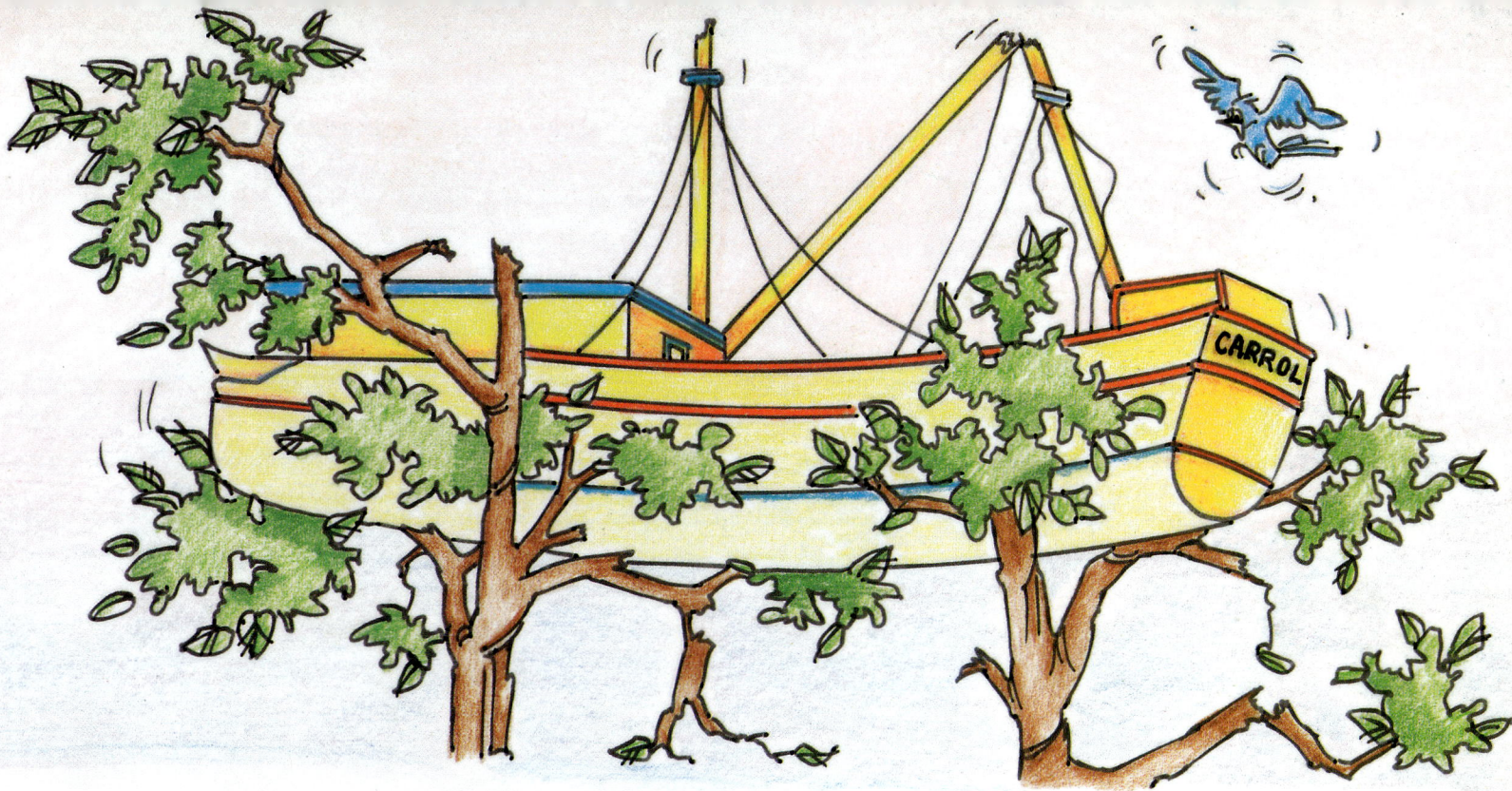

"What's a Category 5 like?" asked Petey, fearfully.

"A Category 5 is the biggest, baddest hurricane there is! My whole body hurts before a Category 5 hurricane comes!" answered Old Gus.

"Wow!" gasped Petey and Tazz.

"I can remember just one Category 5 — Hurricane Camille!" said Old Gus. "Just thinking about it gives me goosebumps," Old Gus shivered and continued, "Camille roared into the Biloxi, Mississippi, area in August 1969. Her winds were as fast as a speeding train — 175 miles an hour. Gigantic waves swept away big hotels, apartment buildings, and homes. Camille tossed ships around like they were toys. Over 250 lives were lost. Camille was no lady! She was one of the worst hurricanes in history."

"For sure!" agreed Tazz.

"Tell us some more about hurricanes!" begged Petey and Tazz.

"Let's see . . . hmm," said Old Gus, thinking, "did I tell you about the tornadoes?"

"What tornadoes?" gasped Petey and Tazz.

"The ones that come from hurricanes," Old Gus said. "A tornado tears up just about everything in its path. Tornadoes can even form over water. They're called waterspouts!"

"Did I tell you that hurricanes can move inland?" asked Old Gus.

"But I thought hurricanes were only dangerous to the coast!" said Petey.

Old Gus shook his head and continued, "No! Hurricanes are a threat inland as well. Hurricane Hugo tore through Charlotte, North Carolina, and Charlotte is 200 miles away from the coast!"

"One good thing nowadays," said Old Gus, "those Weather Service boys do give folks warning before a hurricane comes. Just like when Hurricane Fran hit North Carolina in 1996. They warned that Fran could hit the coast, but no one knew exactly where. From South Carolina all the way up the coast of North Carolina thousands of people evacuated. Fran made landfall near Cape Fear just after midnight on September 6. Her winds topped 100 miles an hour. The storm surge threw cars and boats around."

"Did anyone get hurt?" asked Petey.

"Sadly, yes," answered Old Gus, "but it could have been worse. Due to the advance warning of Fran's coming, preparations were made and many lives were saved."

No Hurricane!

"Is a hurricane coming here?" Petey asked Old Gus.

"Well . . . let's see . . ." Old Gus said, then paused. Old Gus stretched his feet and toes and hopped around. He moved his head from side to side. Finally, he answered, "Nope! I don't have the feeling at all!"

"Thank goodness!" sighed Petey and Tazz, relieved.

"I must be going," said Old Gus. "It was nice to have met you boys."

"Goodbye," said Petey and Tazz. "Thanks for telling us about hurricanes."

"My pleasure!" shouted Old Gus as he flapped his wings and flew away.

Tazz and Petey went back to having fun.

At least for today, there were no hurricanes to worry about!

"Learning about hurricanes sure was exciting!" cried Petey.
"Sure enough!" agreed Tazz. "But time's awastin', Petey My Boy!"
Side by side, their eyes shining with excitement, Petey and Tazz start out on their NEXT
BIG ADVENTURE!

More about Hurricanes . . .

There are no other storms like hurricanes on earth! A hurricane is a type of tropical cyclone (a circulating weather system). A hurricane has a well defined circulation and maximum sustained winds of 74 mph or more.

Hurricanes form over warm tropical oceans. They get their energy from contact with the warm ocean water and the atmosphere. Hurricanes are steered by easterly trade winds, temperate west winds, and their own tremendous energy. In the center of the hurricane, increasingly high winds cause the sea to churn violently. When a hurricane moves ashore it sweeps the ocean water inward over the coastline. Hurricanes spawn tornadoes and cause extremely heavy rains and severe flooding.

Official hurricane season is from June 1 to November 30 for the United States. But most hurricanes hit from mid-August to late October. Each year, around ten tropical storms develop over the Atlantic, the Caribbean, and the Gulf of Mexico. Of these ten storms, six may become hurricanes. About five hurricanes hit the United States every three years, and two will be major hurricanes of Category 3 or higher.

With new technology such as geostationary satellites, reconnaissance aircraft or "hurricane hunters," radar, and computer models, we have been able to give timely warnings of the approach of hurricanes. This has resulted in less deaths than in past years. Because more people live near the coast today, property damage has risen over the years. Hurricanes pose a significant threat to our coastlines and inland as well. Unfortunately, many people do not take the threat of a hurricane seriously. Most people living in areas prone to hurricanes have never experienced the destruction of a "major" hurricane. This leads to a false sense of safety and delayed action when a hurricane does strike. That next hurricane could be the "big" one! Everyone needs to take hurricanes seriously.

Saffir-Simpson Hurricane Scale
(The "Real" Hurricane Scale)

Number (Category)	Sustained Winds (MPH)	Damage	Examples (States Affected)
1	74-95	Minimal	Charley 1988 (NC)
2	96-110	Moderate	Bob 1991 (RI)
3	111-130	Extensive	Emily 1993 (Outer Banks NC)
4	131-155	Extreme	Andrew 1992 (FL)
			Hugo 1989 (SC)
5	156+	Catastrophic	Camille 1969 (LA/MS)

Even more about Hurricanes . . .

What's in a name?

Hurricanes have names because more than one hurricane could be brewing at once. Hurricanes used to be given only women's names. Now they are named after men too.

Some terms . . .

- Tropical Depression — An organized storm system with a defined circulation and maximum sustained winds of 38 mph or less.
- Tropical Storm — An organized storm system with a defined circulation and maximum sustained winds of 39 to 73 mph.
- Storm Surge — A large dome of water 50 to 100 miles wide that sweeps over the coast when a hurricane makes landfall.
- Storm Tide — The combination of the storm surge and normal astronomical tide.

If a Hurricane threatens, **know** these terms . . .

HURRICANE WATCH: Hurricane conditions are possible within the next 36 hours. Prepare to take action!

HURRICANE WARNING: Hurricane conditions are expected within 24 hours. Complete all storm preparations. Evacuate if you are directed to.

Hurricanes have eyes . . . ?

The center of a hurricane is called the "eye." The most violent activity takes place in the eyewall (area immediately around the eye). The eye of a hurricane is calm. The most dangerous part of a hurricane is the right front corner. That part has the strongest wind, the heaviest rains, and the highest waves. After the eye passes, the winds will change direction and quickly return to hurricane force.

About tornadoes . . .

Hurricanes often produce tornadoes. Tornadoes only last a few minutes. They have wind speeds of over 200 mph! Tornadoes can form over water — they are called waterspouts.

If a Hurricane threatens . . .

Don't panic. Remember the National Weather Service will give you advance warning before a Hurricane strikes.

Listen for information. The National Weather Service and the National Hurricane Center will keep you updated and furnish you with instructions.

Complete preparation activities. Secure loose objects, board windows, etc.

Follow instructions by local officials. Leave immediately if told to do so! If you are told to evacuate, leave early. Seek shelter inland or at designated shelters outside the flood zone.

If you live in a mobile home — LEAVE!

Tell your neighbors and family outside of the warned area that you are leaving and what your plans are.

If you cannot take your pet, **please** leave food and water for it.

Be prepared!

- Have batteries, drinking water, canned food, candles, and medication on hand.
- Have a first aid kit and manual!
- Keep vehicles fueled.
- Secure your property and bring all loose articles inside.
- Have extra cash for emergencies.

If you get trapped at home during a Hurricane . . .

- Use common sense!
- Stay away from windows and doors. Take refuge in a small interior room, closet, etc.
- If you are in a two-story house, go to an interior room on the first floor.
- Lie on the floor under a table or sturdy object.
- Stay inside a well constructed building.
- Turn off gas and propane tanks.
- Unplug small appliances.
- Fill a bathtub and large containers with water for later use.
- Turn your refrigerator to the coldest setting and keep closed.

Most of all . . . Be Prepared, Follow local officials orders, Don't Panic, and use Common Sense. Be Safe and Cautious. You never know what a Hurricane will do. **The next one may be the "Big" one.**

The Adventure Continues...

Join Petey & Tazz
on their next
Big Adventure!

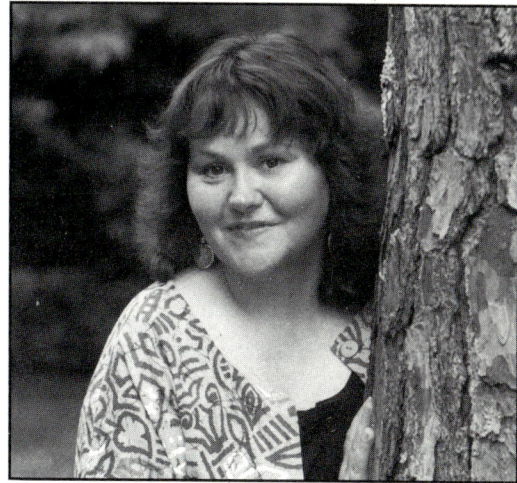

Mary Māden, *Author*

HAVE YOU READ?...

#1 in the series *Flying High With The Wright Brothers*

#2 in the series *The Secret of Blackbeard's Treasure*

#3 in the series *In Search Of The Lost Colony*

#4 in the series *A Lighthouse Adventure*

#5 in the series *Shipwreck!*

#6 in the series *Hurricane!*

#7 in the series *The Great Pirate Adventure*

Also: Look For All My Coloring Books

Look for our next book #8 in the series...

Coming Soon! Look for *Earth / Ocean Adventures—*
An Exciting New Series by Mary Māden!

Dog and Pony Publishing
P.O. Box 3540, Kill Devil Hills, NC 27948
Phone (252) 261-6905

THE ADVENTURE CONTINUES...

Come along on a wild adventure that is guaranteed to blow you away! Get hit by wave after wave of action and fun.

Join Petey, the wild pony, and his best friend Tazz the dog for a day at the Beach. But what happens next is no picnic! See how Petey and Tazz's peaceful day turns into a hair-raising experience when a Hurricane threatens to strike the coast.

Learn all about Hurricanes from the **expert** — a pelican named Old Gus. Find out how Old Gus and those "Weather Service Boys" predict hurricanes. Hear nail-biting accounts of such legendary Hurricanes as **Hazel, Camille, Andrew, Emily,** and even **Fran.** Old Gus's tales of Hurricanes of the past will keep you on the edge of your seat.

Hurricane! is full of facts, thrills, and non-stop excitement. So come along — Be Brave — Let *Hurricane!* sweep you away!

ISBN 1-890479-51-9

90000>

ISBN 1-890479-51-9
$5.95 U.S.

9 781890 479510